Tricia Guild
cut flowers

Photographs by
James Merrell
Text by Elspeth Thompson
and Tricia Guild

Quadrille

for Lily

Tulip *Tulipa* 'Rhapsody'

contents

Love-in-a-mist *Nigella hispanica*
Scabious *Scabiosa caucasica*
Sword lily *Gladiolus iridaceae* 'Fidelio'

wild about flowers

For as long as I can remember, flowers have been a passion and a constant source of inspiration. As a child, I would draw and paint them for hours on end; as an adult, I marvel at their existence. Growing and tending flowers is an important part of my daily life. Wherever I live or work, there are flowers: not grand arrangements, but a few stems – elegant calla lilies in an extraordinary shade of deep magenta, or vibrant saffron nasturtiums picked from the garden – giving soul to the atmosphere.

Flowers have the power to animate a room. Unlike furniture and fabrics, that we choose and change with great deliberation, they are totally spontaneous, filling the

Calla lily *Zantadeschia rehmanii*

space with the energy and unpredictability of the natural world. I particularly enjoy the way in which, in the course of a few days, straight stems and tight buds open to become wonderful, wild and wayward creatures. So often, a flower is at its most beautiful just before it dies. There is much to observe and learn from their natural rhythms and from their generous, unselfconscious beauty.

Since the first days of Designers Guild, flowers have inspired some of my favourite textile designs - the over-sized tulip drawn for us by Howard Hodgkin, Kaffe Fassett's geranium leaves, soft watercoloured tea roses, and the vibrant and exotic colours from the 'Damascena' collection. Even when not graphically present, the colours of flowers are always an influence - the deep cobalt blue of a delphinium spire, pale acid lime alchemilla leaves, and the perfect pinks and oranges of zinnias and gerberas.

Peony *Paeonia lactiflora* cv
African lily *Agapanthus* cv

This book is not about fancy arrangements. You won't find instructions for using florist's wire, or for poking the stems into blocks of oasis. It's about the intense joy and pleasure one can derive from the simple, yet thoughtful arrangement of flowers; the way even a vase of humble narcissi can transform a room, create a mood, revive a flagging spirit. Above all, it's a book about looking at flowers, and about picking and placing them so their strength and fragile beauty can truly be seen. Flowers have the power to make us look at life anew.

Like a flower, which has been through a whole cycle of growth before it blooms in our homes, this book has been a long time in the making. What you see here is a selection from hundreds of photographs taken in all seasons over the course of a year. The result is a personal and passionate view of flowers which I hope will be shared.

Tricia Guild

Lady's mantle *Alchemilla mollis*

Nasturtium *Tropaeolum majus* (Jewel mixed)

A room without flowers

For those who love flowers, a room without them is like a room with the lights out - a room without life. No matter how perfect the decorations, how miraculous the morning light, it will seem somehow soulless without a bowl of tulips by the window, a few stems from the garden by the bed. It is not just their tender, fragile beauty - though what can compare with a peony frilled out in the sun, or the paper-thin petals of an anemone the day before it dies? The presence of flowers in a room goes far deeper than the physical.

For those who love flowers, their rhythms and rituals become part of life itself. The early morning trips to the market, the unwrapping and stripping of the stems, the choice of which vase to use and what colours to set together, right down to the tweaking of the last stem to create the final balance. There is a sensual joy in the rustle of leaves and paper and the feel of the cool, wet stems, the subtle, earthy scent of violets,

is a room without life

or the heady aroma of tuberose. But that's not all. Flowers change every day. Buds open, stems twist and sway, petals drop, and then they die – reminding us of the process of change at work in every aspect of our own lives. Then the cycle starts over again. For those who love flowers find it hard to live without them.

The American writer May Sarton, whose wonderful *Journal of a Solitude* is coloured by the intense and particular joy she finds in having flowers about her house, puts it like this: 'Without them I would die. Why do I say that? Partly because they change before my eyes, they live and die in a few days. They keep me in touch with process, with growth, and also with dying. I am floated on their moments.'

The ephemeral nature of flowers, their aching immediacy, helps us to live in the present. Look at them *now*, see them *this moment* as the light falls on spiralling petals – tomorrow they'll be different, indeed, tomorrow

For those who love flowers, their rhythms

may be too late. Flowers are symbols of spontaneous joy. And yet, at the same time, layered within the experience of the moment, flowers can summon memories of the past. For centuries, and in almost all societies, flowers have been associated with key moments in our lives. They commemorate births, weddings and funerals; they form part of religious rites and ceremonies; they are the time-honoured gift between old friends and new lovers.

Flowers have the power to evoke intense emotions, to encapsulate moods, to flood the heart with the feeling that summed up a conversation, a summer, a marriage, a year. As he was dying, the poet John Keats wrote to a friend: 'I muse with the greatest affection on every flower I have known from my infancy - the shapes and colours are as new to me as if I

and rituals become part of life itself

had just created them with a superhuman fancy. It is because they are connected with the most thoughtless and the happiest moments of our lives.' It might be a bunch of birthday roses, wild flowers picked on holiday and placed in a hotel room window, or the posy of snowdrops placed beside the bed when you stayed with a friend – it's as if the presence of flowers is what actually imprints a memory in our minds. Louis MacNeice understood this when he wrote about an unexpected snowfall:

> The room was suddenly rich and the great bay window was
> Spawning snow and pink roses against it
> Soundlessly collateral and incompatible;
> The world is suddener than we fancy it.

Returning from the market,
unwrapping the flowers and
preparing them, clipping
stems and choosing
containers and vases is
relaxing and creative,
and almost as pleasurable
as seeing them in their
final setting.

Grape hyacinth *Muscari botryoides*

Just a few blooms in a jar can be enough. In fact, the more enormous and elaborate the display, the less one looks at the individual flowers. And the real power of flowers lies in the looking. Those who truly love flowers do not need to contort them into complicated arrangements, to spike them with wires or poke them into mesh or foam. They prefer to let the flowers speak for themselves - just one type of tulip in a plain glass vase, a spray of apple blossom against a bright pink wall, the tiniest posy of garden flowers, cut short and arranged with love in a cup by the bed.

So often, we plunge a bunch of flowers into water with little further thought or attention. We haven't the time, we say; we're no good with flowers. And the flowers will be beautiful all the same. But a little extra effort reaps infinite rewards. Arranging flowers is a deeply personal creative process in which the flowers, the vase, the setting and one's own mood and inclination each play a vital part. The same flowers can create a completely different effect depending on the vase used, the length the stems are cut, the scale of the arrangement, the way the light falls on it, the place where it is put. Flowers can create a mood that is sensual, romantic, cheerful, peaceful or energizing. They can be magical, modern, challenging, mysterious. They always heighten the atmosphere.

Certain arrangements will be a dominant presence - a bowl of dark calla lilies on a central table, or a billowing armful of lilacs that fills the whole room with its scent. Others may subtly inhabit a shelf, sidetable or windowsill - not apparent at first glance, but discovered in good time. Smaller flowers work well when grouped with a few little objects in a vignette. A bunch of grape hyacinths, which would have no impact in a large room, becomes an intimate offering on a small table with a framed photograph, a candlestick and a favourite book. Follow your intuition. Breathe in their beauty. Watch them well - and listen.

To be appreciated in all their richness, flowers need to be looked at. Each one is a wonder, and not to be wasted. Take time in the picking of them, the choosing of the vase, the placing in water, the setting of the vase in the room. And most of all, take time to look at them as they live out their lives in a few days before you. Let their tender beauty invade your life. In the words of an artist who painted flowers all her life:

Still

in a way

nobody sees a flower

really

it is so small

we haven't the time

and to see takes time

like to have a friend

takes time.

Georgia O'Keeffe

Horsetail
Equisetum arvense

Barberton daisy
Gerbera jamesonii
'Sundance'

Earth

laughs in

flowers.

Ralph Waldo
Emerson

Anemone
coronaria cv

Hyacinth
Hyacinthus
orientalis cv

joy

Flowers can be the purest expression of joy in a house. In particular, they can raise the spirits on entering. Have flowers in the hall that make you feel glad to come home. The bright, pure beauty of gerberas looks particularly joyful against a coloured wall — and the wild, painterly patterns of parrot tulips have all the energy of an artist's brush. In other rooms, place flowers where a sudden shaft of sunlight will illuminate the petals. Even on the dullest winter's day, flowers are a sign of life and hope and sheer exuberance.

Parrot tulips, their crinkled petals just opening, form a ring of fiery red around the rim of the blue container, against which the deeper blue of delphinium spires can sing out. Gloriosas and a single dahlia add a note of quirky spontaneity.

Tulip *Tulipa* (Parrot Group) 'Roccoco'
Glory lily *Gloriosa superba* 'Rothschildiana'
Dahlia cv
Delphinium (Belladonna Group) 'Blue Bees'

Bellflower *Campanula
carpatica*

Cow parsley *Anthriscus
sylvestris*

Lily-of-the-valley
Convallaria majalis

I find the scent of certain flowers, such as lily of the valley, can evoke an intense feeling of well-being. In other flowers, such as cow parsley or lady's lace, it is the textures - light and frothy and infused with sunshine - that raise the spirits. I picked these flowers from a glorious lakeside garden in Sweden.

Choosing the right container can create an interesting harmony between the beautiful handmade ceramic or glass vase and the flower you place in it. Pink zinnias, a rose and individual blooms plucked from a spire of gladiolus form an unexpectedly joyful combination; a lime green alchemilla leaf echoes the acid green of the tiny handmade pot.

Zinnia elegans
'Border Beauty Rose'

Rosa rugosa
'Roseraie de l'Haÿ'

Sword lily
Gladiolus 'Fidelio'
iridaceae

simplicity

Sometimes a single bloom can say it all. The secret of arranging flowers does not lie in size or quantity. It is in the sensitive bringing together of all the elements – flowers, water, leaves, vase, materials – so that the purest qualities of the blooms can sing out. The beauty of a single blue delphinium flower can be seen in all its perfection against a simple white ceramic pot. When using a mass of flowers, try keeping to one or two colours. Learn how less can be more. The graduated blues, mauves and indigoes of larkspur or delphinium are set off by the dull bluish hue of galvanized metal against a textured blue wall.

Delphinium
elatum
'Faust'

Delphinium (Belladonna Group) 'Blue Bees'

I chose these swaying stems
of wild lupin and eremurus as
they relate so well to the
flowing design of the curtain
fabric. In this simple
arrangement, the flowers and
the foliage, the graphic glass
vase and the quality of light
in the room all come together
to create a mood of calm and
intimacy - contemporary
lifestyle in an old setting.

A grey day ... but, strangely enough,

a grey day makes the bunches of flowers

in the house have a particular

radiance, a kind of pure white light.

May Sarton

Lupin *Lupinus polyphyllus*
Foxtail lily *Eremurus stenophyllus*

African lily *Agapanthus* cv

Allium giganteum

Fennel *Foeniculum vulgare*

Stems, leaves, individual petals and

Zinnia elegans
Decorative dahlia *Dahlia* cv
Arum leaf *Zantadeschia aethiopica*

stamens each have their own loveliness

Red hot
poker
Kniphofia cv

modernity

Flowers in themselves are neither old-fashioned nor new. Like clothes, it is the way in which they are used that lets them be seen in new ways. Displayed singly, in a simple glass vase, even traditional, cottage-garden flowers such as pansies, nasturtiums and love-in-a-mist can be seen in all their startling, sculptural beauty. Gerberas or cultivated orchids have the graphic impact of an abstract painting. Be brave. Use clashing colours. Play with patterns and textures. The boldest blooms will stand out against the brightest colours.

the graphic impact of

Barberton daisy *Gerbera jamesonii*

an abstract painting

Flowers with strong,
sculptural shapes look
particularly effective
against the coloured
plaster walls in our
dining room. Elegant
arum lilies and
montbretia seedheads
complement the hand-made
glass vases, the rough,
raw wood of the table
and the raffia chairs.

stem, bud and twig

Arum lily
Zantadeschia aethiopica

Montbretia *Crocosmia* cv

two by two

Belladonna lily *Amaryllis belladonna*

There's a commonly held idea that you should only use flowers in odd numbers. In my view, they can look just as special and more contemporary used in pairs.

The simpler and more
pared-down the
arrangement, the more
crucial balance becomes.
Regardless of where I
begin working with
flowers, the final
adjustments are carried
out in situ. Like
painting a picture,
arranging flowers is a
process of adding and
subtracting, simply and
with feeling, until the
result feels right.

Delphinium elatum 'Crystal'
Allium giganteum

Pansy
Viola cv

sensuality

Flowers appeal to senses other than sight. Breathing deep from the innermost petals of a rose, or entering a room in which lilies have been shut all night, are experiences that never pall in their impact. Some flowers are generous with their scent, filling a whole house in an hour; for others, such as lily of the valley, you have to move in close. The texture of flowers provides endless pleasures – from the rustle of leaves as the paper is unwrapped and the feel of the cold wet stems under water, to the contrasting qualities of the petals.

heady fragrance

Lily-of-the-valley *Convallaria majalis*

To be overpowered by

the fragrance of flowers is

a delectable form of defeat.

Beverly Nichols

The true
mystery of
the world is
the visible
not the
invisible.

Oscar Wilde

Arum leaf
Zantadeschia aethiopica

voluptuous curves

Dahlia cv

Arum leaf
Zantadeschia
aethiopica

dark trumpets

Like a jazz song
I can't forget
all my friends
and lovers
who gave me flowers.

Bruce Weber

Calla lily *Zantadeschia rehmanii* cv

Her big, lewd, bold eye

in its sooty lashes . . .

Ted Hughes *Big Poppy*

Oriental poppy *Papaver orientalis*

mystery

Flowers are everyday miracles. They connect us with the subtle currents of nature, with what Dylan Thomas called 'the force that through the green fuse drives the flower'. Perhaps the best way to appreciate the wonder of a flower is to try to imagine ourselves as children. The American ecologist Rachel Carson wrote of the need to keep the 'clear-eyed vision, that true instinct for what is beautiful and awe-inspiring' with which children look at the natural world, the 'sense of wonder so indestructible that it would last throughout life'.

Streptocarpus
leaf

I'm passionate about
mauve - its mood of
mystery and seduction.
Lupins forming their
own patterns, their
mauves and blues
heightening the other
colours in the room,
capture the first
moments of summer.

Lupin *Lupinus polyphyllus*

We cannot
fathom the
mystery of a
single flower.
Nor is it
intended that
we should.

John Ruskin

They change before my eyes, they
live and die in a few days. They
keep me in touch with process, with
growth, and also with dying.
I am floated on their moments.

May Sarton

Nasturtium *Tropaeolum majus* (Gleam series)

Putting an eye
too close,
until it blurs,
You see a
firmament, a
ring of sky,
With a white
radiance in it,
a universe,
And something
there that
might seem to
sing or fly.

Ruth Pitter

Triteleia laxa
'Koningin Fabiola'

translucence

Water forms part of the essential elemental nature of flowers: they rise out of the earth, draw water up their stems, move and breathe in the air and open their petals to the fiery sun. It was its perfect embodiment of the four elements that made the lotus the ultimate spiritual flower in ancient Eastern scriptures. Water is as integral a part of a flower arrangement as the vase. It reminds us that flowers are living things - even glossy tulips or candy-pink gerberas, which can seem almost plastic in their perfection.

Cyclamen
persicum

Stems in water reflect the
iridescent indigo colour
behind, echoing one's image of
the ocean's depths, and are as
much a part of the arrangement
as the sweet-scented garden
roses above them.

Rosa rugosa 'Roseraie de l'Haÿ'

Cactus dahlia *Dahlia* cv

The flowers... were suddenly there,
shivering swimmers on the edge of a gala
- nude whites and yellows shocking the raw air.
They'd switched themselves on like streetlamps.

Carol Rumens

Cactus dahlia *Dahlia* cv

Nasturtium leaf *Tropaeolum majus*

Hydrangea quercifolia leaf

Five individual flowers in
identical containers form
a spontaneous dancing
group. I like the playful
simplicity of plain glass
bottles, water and stems.

Calendula officinalis

Iceland
poppy
Papaver
nudicaule

stillness

Flowers invite us to slow down, to take the time to 'stop and stare'. Like the lilies of the field in the Bible, they remind us that true peace and beauty are not dependent on what we wear, what we eat, what work we do or even whom we love. Their brief lives - from tight bud to blown petals in a few days - have the power to bring our busy minds back to the here and now. A few blooms on the desk where you work can aid concentration and encourage contemplation. Watch and pray. To look long and deep into the face of a flower is a modern-day meditation.

Flowers hold a life within

of their own.

I learned that flowers talk;

I learned to listen

Walter Hubert

Allium aflatunense

Armfuls of lilac in so many
different shades, their
stems cleaned and drenched
with lots of water, create
a cloud of fragrance in a
calm white space.

With many a pointed blossom

rising delicate, with the

perfume strong I love

With every leaf a miracle

Walt Whitman
Leaves of Grass

Lilac *Syringa vulgaris*

Zinnia elegans (Big Top series)

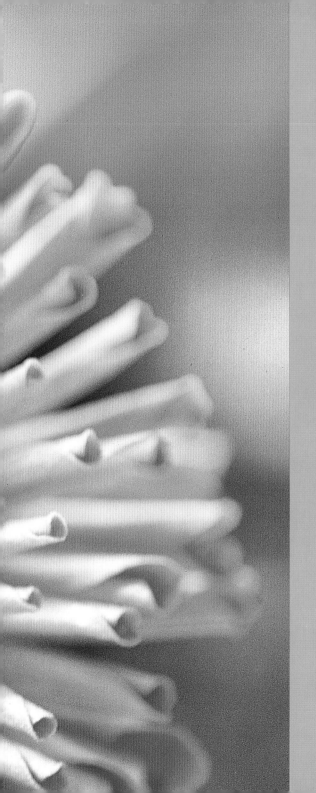

spontaneity

Even familiar flowers can sometimes surprise, causing us to look at them with new eyes. Playing games with scale makes us do a double-take. Mix flowers of different sizes – alliums, anemones, the tiniest grape hyacinths – in the same vase. Or try changing the context – garden flowers such as pelargoniums, pansies and morning glory are seldom used as cut flowers and this increases their impact.

Tulip Tulipa "Appledoorn"

Barberton daisy
Gerbera jamesonii

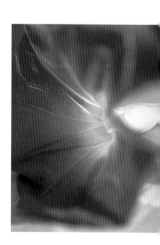

Pansy *Viola* cv   *Verbena* cv   Morning glory *Ipomoea purpurea*

Some wild flowers may last only a few hours but, used sparingly, give extraordinary pleasure, perhaps because of their fragility. Pick a morning glory and float it on a leaf for a summer lunch table.

Scarlet fever

Pot geranium *Pelargonium*

abstract beauty

To see only the flower is to miss half the beauty. Stems, leaves, individual petals and stamens each have their own loveliness. Take time to take in the texture of a leaf, the pattern of the veins and its silver underside. See how the chocolate-brown stems of pink nerines throw graphic shadows against a wall. Place flowers where they can be seen from more than one side and enjoy the play of light and shade against different backdrops. Like a Cubist painter, home in on distinct parts of the plant at different angles. Look and look again. There is always more to see.

African lily
Agapanthus cv

People from a planet without
flowers would think we must be mad
with joy the whole time to have
such things about us.

Iris Murdoch

Tulip *Tulipa* 'Parade'

Chocolate brown stems

Orchid-lipped, loose-jointed, purplish, indolent flowers,
with a ripe smell of peaches, like a girl's breath through lipstick...
fragrance too rich for keeping, too light to remember...

Anne Stevenson

Moth orchid *Phalaenopsis* cv
Miltoniopsis cv

I find orchids exotic and intriguing. Their abstract sculptural beauty and graphic strength boldly stand out against a painterly flowered background.

Amaryllis

Hippeastrum 'Chrysalis'

Fennel

Foeniculum vulgare

Iceland poppy

Papaver nudicaule

energy

A flower is a living thing, bringing the vibrations of the natural world into your home. Different flowers have different moods and energies. Learn to discriminate between them. With their bright colours and neat, radiating petals, dahlias almost always look cheerful. Black calla lilies are sultry and sensual. Small posies of garden flowers create a mood of intimacy, while feathery cow parsley adds lightness and romance. Bold arrangements of a few bright blooms can raise the energy in a basement or dark hallway.

Iceland
poppy
*Papaver
nudicaule*

Childlike innocence
draped without pretence
unable to provide
anything but unashamed beauty.

Peter Bosch

Zinnia *Zinnia elegans* cv
Cactus dahlia *Dahlia* cv

Flowers have a life and rhythm of their own. Here, garden nasturtiums
and delicate leaves in softly coloured glass vases appear to dance along
a stone chimney and welcome you into the room.

Nasturtium *Tropaeolum majus* 'Tom Thumb'

Flowers, to my thinking, are not merely pretty-pretty. They have in their fragrance an earthiness of the humus and the corruptive earth from which they spring... And pansies, in their streaked faces, have a look of many things besides heartsease.

D H Lawrence *Pansies*

Pansy *Viola* cv
Verbena cv

Barberton daisy
Gerbera jamesonii
'Flolilli' and Germini
'Sardana'

energy

love

In classical times, roses were sacred to Aphrodite, goddess of love. They were the symbol of courtly love in medieval Europe and have been associated with romance ever since. But all flowers are signs of love. 'Love smiled in a flower', wrote the poet Algernon Charles Swinburne of love-in-a-mist. Flowers open our hearts to beauty, which in turn can open us to love. Watching a tulip opening in the sun, experiencing its generous beauty, can create a similar opening in ourselves. Whether for yourself or for another, flowers are about love. Choose and arrange your blooms with love and care.

Rosa rugosa
'Roseraie
de l'Haÿ'

When the heart is open

you will change

just like a flower slowly opening.

Van Morrison

Tulip *Tulipa* 'Attila' and 'Blenda'

*Anemone
coronaria* cv

Delphinium
(Belladonna
Group)
'Guinevere'

*Allium
giganteum*

Chocolate cosmos *Cosmos atrosanguineus*

Sometimes, shaping bread or scraping potatoes for supper,

I have stood in the kitchen, transfixed by what I'd call

love if love were a whiff, a wanting for no particular

lover, no child, or baby or creature. 'Love, dear love'

I could cry to these scent-spilling ragged flowers.

Anne Stevenson

purity

The beauty of flowers is completely unself-conscious. The photographer Peter Bosch likened photographing flowers to photographing children, referring to their 'childlike innocence, draped without pretence, unable to pose, yet unable to provide anything but unashamed beauty'. You do not need to dress a flower up to make it lovely. To look into its face is to behold the purity at the heart of nature, to believe once again in a god of small things.

Narcissus
'Geranium'

Un fiore bianco, di amore irresistibile.

Pablo Neruda

Arum lily *Zantadeschia aethiopica*

Isolated from the
hedgerow or the bunch
of cottage flowers, a
single bloom of scabious
or love-in-a-mist
becomes sculptural and
sophisticated within a
minimal setting. I often
remove the leaves to
give a clearer shape.

Love-in-a-mist
Nigella hispanica

Scabious
Scabiosa caucasica
'Clive Greaves'

With a pure colour there is little one can do

Of a pure thing there is little one can say.

We are dumb in the face of that cold blush of blue,

Called glory, and enigmatic as the face of day.

Ruth Pitter *Morning Glory*

Morning glory *Ipomoea purpurea*

The translucent
quality of the two
pink poppies gives a
shock of contrast to
the soft blues and
mauves of my
bedroom, lifting my
spirits on waking.

A man who takes great pleasure in flowers
will always be reminded of his own fragility.

Horti Itzeinensis

Iceland poppy *Papaver nudicaule*
Sweet peas *Lathyrus odoratus* cv
Love-in-a-mist *Nigella hispanica*

flower glossary

General Care Notes
Never put cut flowers
into a vase of water
without first cutting the
stems. Always make sure
the receptacle is
spotlessly clean: plants
exude and leave a residue
which in time becomes a
bacterial 'slime.' This
slime will stay behind in
the vase, even if the
water is changed, and
will reduce the lifespan
of any new flower placed
in that vase. Before
using, scrub out the vase
using a capful of bleach;
minute particles of
bleach do not harm
flowers and can actually
help them live longer.
The best method of
enhancing the life of any
flower is to wash out the
vase in between use, keep
the water clean, and top
up regularly with cold,
clean water.

Preparation
Remove all foliage that
will be submerged in
water; otherwise it will
decay and cause bacteria
to grow, which will
shorten the length of the
flowers' life. With roses
it is also advisable to
run a sharp florist's
knife down the stems to
remove the lower thorns
and avoid ripping other
flower stems.

AGAPANTHUS *Alliaceae*
African lily
Available most of the year
but best in the summer
months. Colour range from
white, pale blue—to deep
blue. Do not buy with
flowers too open. Look for
'dried—out' buds. Check for
dropping. See care notes.

ALCHEMILLA MOLLIS *Rosaceae*
Lady's mantle or fool's gold
Available in the summer.
Lovely, light, frothy,
acid green sprays of tiny
flowers surrounded by
whorls of pretty, rounded,
wavy light green leaves.
When drops of dew get
trapped in the leaf center
they glisten like jewels,
hence the old wife's term
'fool's gold.' See care
notes.

ALLIUM *Alliaceae*
Ornamental onion
A. aflatunense
Available summer only.
Heads not so dense or
globular as *A. giganteum*
although still strongly
smelling of onions. Lighter
in colour and appearance.
See care notes.

A. giganteum
Available summer only.
Large round purple flower
heads. Long lasting. Strong
onion aroma, so better not
mixed with sweet—smelling
flowers. See care notes.

AMARYLLIS *Amaryllidaceae*
Belladonna lily
Available late summer and
autumn and occasionally
at other times of the
year. Long lasting
clusters of trumpet—
shaped flowers in shades
of rose-pink. There is
also a white form. See
care notes.

ANEMONE CORONARIA
Ranunculaceae
Available all year but
not best in summer
months. De Caen group
produces wonderful, large
'velvety' blooms of
cerise reds and purple.
White available also,
though not as good. If
floppy when bought, place
in deep cold water to
revive quickly. Quite
long lasting.

ANTHRISCUS SYLVESTRIS
Apiaceae
Cow parsley or lady's lace
Available almost
everywhere in gardens and
waysides during late
April to June. Soft,
fluffy umbels of tiny,
white flowers in
profusion. After picking,
strip off all foliage and
place immediately in warm
water. Leave for 12
hours and then top up
with cold water. Not very
long lasting, but
extremely pretty.

CALENDULA OFFICINALIS
Asteraceae
Available most of the year
but best in the summer.
Good cut flower with
sunny, bright orange and
gold 'face.' Pale yellow
variety has recently been
introduced. All parts of
the plant have a pleasant
distinctive aroma. Make
sure all lower foliage is
removed, or the water will
smell. See care notes.

CAMPANULA CARPATICA
Campanulaceae
Bellflower
A low-growing rock garden
variety not available as a
cut flower. The blue-purple
cup-shaped flowers appear
in July and August. Pick
and immediately place in
water. Not long lasting.

CONVALLARIA MAJALIS
Convallariaceae
Lily-of-the-valley
Available almost all the
year but expensive unless
bought in season in May.
Available growing in pots.
Famous, characteristically
sweet scent. See care notes.

COSMOS *Asteraceae*
C. bipinnatus
Annual cosmos
Available throughout the
summer and early autumn.
Single dahlia-like flowers
produced in a wide range
of colours.

. atrosanguineus
chocolate cosmos.
This perennial variety is a
delicious new cut flower —a
rich, velvety brown red.
Long-lasting cut flowers on
long, strong, slim stems.
See care notes.

CROCOSMIA *Iridaceae*
Montbretia
Available late summer to
autumn. Tubular blooms of
lemon, burnt orange, and
red are carried on
strongly zigzagged
branching stems. As
flowers drop they leave
behind attractively shaped
seed pods which give a
wonderfully graphic
effect. See care notes.

CYCLAMEN PERSICUM
Primulaceae
Available as potted plants
in autumn and winter only.
Colour range: white, soft
pink cerise, and red. Some
variations of the white
and pink are delicately
scented. Cut stems off
plant to enjoy the clarity
of the flower on its own.
Keep cool. Not very long
lasting when cut.

DAHLIA *Asteraceae*
Decorative dahlia
Cactus dahlia
Available summer and early
autumn. Broad spectrum of
varieties and colours.
Single double pompon and
spiky 'cactus' blooms. The
dahlia is enjoying a
modern revival as a
bright, showy, long
lasting cut-flower. The

best 'mixes' can still be
found at roadside stalls.
See care notes.

DELPHINIUM *Ranunculaceae*
Available most of the
year. The Belladonna
group are smaller and
more branched than
Delphinium elatum and
sometimes called the
'Butterfly delphinium.'
Look for varieties such
as 'Blue Bees' and
'Wendy.' True good blues.
Strip off all lower
leaves. See care notes.

D. elatum hybrids
Available most of the
year. Best May through to
August. Large, erect with
large, full, flat flowers.
Colour range from pure
white to soft lilacs
and pinks to pale
blue and indigo
with white, cream, and
black eye. Royal and
impressive blooms.
Extra care tip: hold with
stem upside down and fill
hollow with cold water.
Plug with absorbent cotton.

EQUISETUM ARVENSE
Equisetaceae
Horsetail or Snakegrass
One of the oldest plants
on the planet. Stems
available most of the
year. See care notes.

EREMURUS STENOPHYLLUS
Asphodelaceae
Foxtail lily
Available late spring and
summer. Majestic spires of
star-shaped flowers from

white, cream yellow
through orange. Good cut
flower with similar
'moving' feature as the
lupin. See care notes.

FOENICULUM VULGARE
Apiaceae
Fennel
Late summer and autumn.
The type available
commercially is more
likely to be the 'Golden
Dill' from Holland
(*Anethum graveolens*). Both
have a pleasant aniseed
smell and pretty parasols
of tiny gold florets with
soft, feathery foliage.
See care notes.

GERBERA JAMESONII
Asteraceae
Barberton daisy or
Transvaal daisy
Available all year in a
wide range of vibrant and
pastel colours. There is
also a smaller-headed
form known as 'Germina.'
If purchased from a
florist, gerberas will
have been properly
conditioned, but should
the heads be floppy,
treat as follows: drop
each stem through a
piece of wire netting
or a cake rack to support
the head, and leave for
24 hours in tepid
water to firm up then
arrange as usual.

GLADIOLUS *Iridaceae*
Sword lily
Different varieties
available throughout the
year. Look for unusual

'butterfly' type and the
smaller varieties such as
'Nymph.' 'Woodpecker' is a
good green one. Buy as
budded as possible. See
care notes.

GLORIOSA SUPERBA
Colchicaceae
Glory lily
Available all the year.
Exotic tropical lily.
Handle with care as very
delicate, otherwise treat
as usual. Quite long
lasting in spite of its
delicacy.

HIPPEASTRUM *Amaryllidaceae*
Amaryllis
One named variety or
another available through
the year. Popular during
winter and spring months.
This is commonly known as
amaryllis, though that
name properly applies to a
genus of fall-flowering
garden bulbs.

Colours range from pure white and peach to pinks, reds, and multicolours, with flowers ranging from dainty to huge. For long life put a thin plant cane up the hollow stem to the end and cut to length. Fill hollow stem with water and plug with absorbent cotton.

HYACINTHUS ORIENTALIS
Hyacinthaceae
Hyacinth
Available late winter and spring only. White, cream, pink, and blue distinctive, strongly scented blooms. Last longer as pots of bulbs. Handle with extreme care as cut flower. Rinse off soil or sand from stems and avoid cutting, as the sap exuded from the cut stems can cause skin irritations. If in doubt, wear gloves.

IPOMOEA PURPUREA
Convolvulaceae
Morning glory
Not available commercially, but well worth seeking out. Easily grown as a climbing plant in warm and sheltered areas. Trumpet-shaped blooms in clear colours of blue, purple, or pink. As a cut bloom, life expectancy is only a few hours.

KNIPHOFIA CAULESCENS
Asphodelaceae
Red hot poker or torch lily Available summer through early autumn. Vibrant lemon to deep orange, flame-headed spikes. Very graphic and modern. Not very long lasting. See care notes.

LATHYRUS ODORATUS
Papilionaceae
Sweet pea
Early varieties available from late spring through to July. New strains are treated especially for long life. Lovely colours and wonderful scent. See care notes.

LUPINUS *Papilionaceae*
Lupine
Available summer only. A true 'cottage garden' flower. Variety of colours and multicolours. Stems hollow and can be treated like delphiniums. Floral spikes move in a wave-like fashion over a period of 24 hours, giving a delightful effect of movement. See care notes.

MILTONIOPSIS *Orchidaceae*
Available all year round as a small potted plant but not as a cut flower. Similar in appearance to *Phaleanopsis* but smaller. Follow supplier's care instructions. Flowers are very long lasting.

MUSCARI *Hyacinthaceae*
Grape hyacinth
Available late winter through to late May only. Delightful small spires of tiny bells, pale blue to deep blue, though there are more uncommon white forms. Lasts well. See care notes.

NARCISSUS *Amaryllidaceae*
True spring flowers, though some early varieties are available mid-December onward. Many are highly scented, especially the smaller multi-headed forms. Whites and all manner of yellows and golds, some with orange and red eyes. Stems split and curl, so good idea to put clear tape around stems if visible. Keep water clean. See care notes.

NIGELLA HISPANICA
Ranunculaceae
Love-in-a-mist
Available late spring to early autumn. Best known variety is the medium and dark blue, but comes in white, pink, and lilac shades. Soft and delicate appearance. Ripened seed pods are also

attractive. Strip most foliage off, or it will become black, smelly, and slimy.

PAEONIA *Paeoniaceae*
Peony
Available in May through to June only. Beautifully showy when in full bloom. Not many colours produced for the cut flower trade as yet. Look for a show of colour rather than buying in tight bud. Condition in warm water for 24 hours before placing in vase.

PAPAVER *Papaveraceae*
P. nudicaule
Iceland Poppy
Available all the year round. Iceland poppies have a stunning neon colour range and translucency of petal. Stems are already singed, so do not cut unless necessary, but if you do, stems should be re-singed by putting the base of the stem in a naked flame for approximately five seconds to seal in the plant's juices before placing in cool water. Best bought in bud.

P. orientale
Oriental Poppy
Available only direct from the garden. After picking, stems need to be 'seared' if you want them to last. Otherwise, just place in vase of warm water and enjoy the flower's brief life.

PELARGONIUM *Geraniaceae*
Geranium
Available as a summer-flowering pot-grown perennial. Broad selection of vivid and pastel colours from white to black-red. Flower heads will last quite well as a cut flower. See care notes.

PHALAENOPSIS *Orchidaceae*
Moth orchid
Available throughout the year as cut flowers and potpot plants. Long, pendant spikes of flattish blooms in white and strong pink. Elegant and intriguing with long-lasting qualities. They come as cut flowers in a vial of clean water, so remove stem and just transfer to a vase of cool, clean water.

ROSA RUGOSA *Rosaceae*
Rose
This particular rose is a common garden shrub and hedging variety, strong in habit and colour. Pick and treat as for bought roses, which are available all year round in a vast range of type and colour. When buying, look for heads that have broken from the bud and are firm to the touch, with long straight stems and fresh, green unspotted leaves. Cut as usual, taking care not to crush stems. Strip off all lower foliage and place in tepid water up to three-quarters of the stem and give a long drink. If any

heads droop, the whole flower can be revitalized by recutting and laying horizontally in a bath for 6-8 hours.

SCABIOSA *Caucasica*
Dipsacaceae
Scabious
Available late spring through to autumn. Best in summer. Excellent cut flower. Both blue and white available. When buying, look for bright green center and with no stamen yet obvious. See care notes.

SYRINGA *Oleaceae*
Lilac
Available winter into summer but at its best in spring. Fragrant panicles of white, pale mauve, or purple on a long woody stem. Place in warm water with special food supplied on purchase. If heads droop, add hotter water. Do not crush stem ends.

TRITELEIA LAXA
Amaryllidaceae
Available in summer months. Large loose umble of funnel-shaped deep to pale purple-blue flowers on delicate stems. Quite long lasting. See care notes.

TROPAEOLUM MAJUS
Tropaeolaceae
Nasturtium
Another true 'cottage garden' flower, available only direct from the garden. Not grown for the cut flower trade. The

blooms are strangely scented, and the leaves and stems when crushed have a strong, pungent smell. The circular, wavy-edged leaves are equally attractive. An ever-increasing range of gold, orange, and red blooms. Not long lasting.

TULIPA *Liliaceae*
Tulip
Available during winter and spring seasons. An overwhelming range of colour and varieties, from the tiny baby tulips to the fantastic distorted parrots. Part of the particular charm of tulips must be their 180° 'dance.' Each day they are in a different position. Strip off excess foliage, tie up bunch, and place in cold water for at least 6 hours to 'crisp up' after purchase.

VERBENA *Verbenaceae*
Available as summer-flowering container-grown perennials. Hybrids have flowers in vibrant or soft shades of carmine, pinks, mauves, and blues, sometimes with a white eye. Heads last quite well as cut flowers. See care notes.

VIOLA *Violaceae*
Pansy
Available only in pots during winter and summer. Vast and intriguing colour combinations, its little 'face' offering an old-

fashioned charm. Not lasting as a cut flower but all the more beautiful for that brief pleasure.

ZANTEDESCHIA *Araceae*
Z. aethiopica
Arum lily
Easter lily
Available all year round. Best in spring. Classic, cool, elegant spathe of white. The spear-shaped leaves are the perfect foil. Lasts well. After cutting, wrap a piece of clear tape around the stem to prevent splitting and curling. Keep water clean. Look for 'Green Goddess,' a green and cream sister of the grand Arum.

Z. rehmannii and hybrids
Calla lily
Available as above. The flower spathe and stems are smaller than on their grand cousin. Exotic, deep ambers, golds, plums, pinks, and an almost black red are among the exciting colour range. See care notes.

ZINNIA ELEGANS *Asteraceae*
Available from mid-spring to early autumn. Beautiful range of colours. Good 'lastability.' Look for double forms, especially the acid green 'Envy.' Watch for tell-tale 'browning' under heads when purchasing, as this means they are old.

Calla lily *Zantadeschia rehmanii*

acknowledgments

Many thanks and much appreciation to our
very special team: James Merrell, Elspeth
Thompson, Meryl Lloyd, Jo Willer, Lisa Guild,
Anne Furniss and all those involved at
Designers Guild and Quadrille.

Also to Nikki Tibbles at Wild at Heart for
some glorious flowers.

Tricia Guild

Vases, containers, fabrics
and accessories from
Designers Guild Store
267-277 Kings Road
London SW3 5BN

For a list of Designers Guild
stockists and product information:
Tel: 0171 243 7300
Fax: 0171 243 7320

First published in 1998 by
Quadrille Publishing Limited
Alhambra House
27-31 Charing Cross Road
London WC2H 0LS

Reprinted 1998

First paperback edition 2000

Publishing Director Anne Furni
Design Meryl Lloyd
Tricia Guild's Creative
Assistant Jo Willer
Flower Glossary Sandy James
Production Vincent Smith,
                Candida Jackson

British Library Cataloguing in
Publication Data
A catalogue record for this bo
is available from the British
Library

ISBN 1 902757 44 0

Printed and bound in Singapore
by KHL Printing

Cyclamen persicum